T0381143

LIZZIE AND THE SHELTER KITTY
(A TRUE STORY)

& SKIPPY SAVES THE DAY
(A FICTIONAL TALE)

DIANE ELIZABETH KELLEHER

AuthorHouse™
1663 Liberty Drive
Bloomington, IN 47403
www.authorhouse.com
Phone: 833-262-8899

Because of the dynamic nature of the Internet, any web addresses or links contained in this book may have changed since publication and may no longer be valid. The views expressed in this work are solely those of the author and do not necessarily reflect the views of the publisher, and the publisher hereby disclaims any responsibility for them.

Any people depicted in stock imagery provided by Getty Images are models, and such images are being used for illustrative purposes only. Certain stock imagery © Getty Images.

This book is printed on acid-free paper.

ISBN: 979-8-8230-1851-7 (sc)
ISBN: 979-8-8230-1852-4 (e)

Library of Congress Control Number: 2023922722

Print information available on the last page.

Published by AuthorHouse 12/13/2023

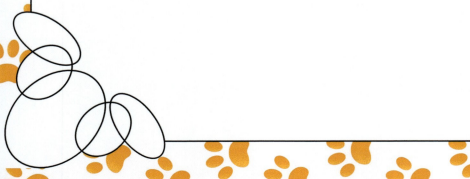

LIZZIE AND THE SHELTER KITTY

(A TRUE STORY)

In memoriam - for all the kitties I have loved -

Libby, died age 20,

Tia, died age 19,

Charlie, died age 11.

And for my darling, beloved Skippy, now age 14.

Lizzie and the Shelter Kitty

There once was a young girl named Lizzie,
Who just love, love, loved little kitties.
And who had a handsome cat named Charlie,
Who was mostly good, but sometimes snarly.

Now, Lizzie had a medical need,
To take her medication every day,
For she suffered from sadness unrelentingly,
Except when with Charlie she played.

Now, Charlie was getting along in years,
Yes, Charlie was getting old.
And one day, he refused to play,
His fate now being foretold.

Charlie had just a sniffle and sneeze,
A dry cough and a little wheeze,
So Lizzie and Laurie, her mother,
Took Charlie to a vet like no other.
Who conducted a multitude of tests.

Now, Charlie did not have a cold,
Lizzie and Laurie were gently told,
No, something else was what was wrong, the vet said:
"Something is wrong inside his head.
Charlie has cancer of the nose."

"Can he be cured?" young Lizzie cried,
Tears streaming down her face.
"Unfortunately, no." the vet replied.
"He's only got a few days!"
And in a few days, poor Charlie died.
And Lizzie and Laura cried, and cried.

And Grandma said, "You're so forlorn,
It's going to take a long time to mourn,
Your dear, dear Charlie - dearly departed."

"No, no" Laurie sighed.
"I have something else in mind,
Because just look at Lizzie's eyes,
So sad, so many tears she's cried."

"Come with me Lizzie we'll take a ride."
"To where?" Miss Lizzie sadly sighed.
"You'll see. I've something good in mind.
You never know just what you'll find."

And to Lizzie's surprise, they took a ride,
Down - to the local animal shelter,
Where kitties were roaming all around,
All around helter-skelter!

Now, one little kitty caught Lizzie's eye,
Because he seemingly had a crooked smile,
A smile aimed just at her,
And when she got close, she could hear his purr.

So, "Who is this kitty" Lizzie asked.
"Oh, that is little Wesley."
"Wesley! What kind of name is that
for a handsome orange tiger cat?"
Lizzie whispered to her mother.
"Why if he were mine,
I would call him "Skippy" and no other."

So Lizzie picked up Skippy,
to hold him as her own,
when she noticed again, his crooked smile,
and finally learned the reason why. You see -
Skippy had periodontal disease, so
Now Skippy has absolutely - NO TEETH!

"Skippy needs to take his medication daily"
the smiling veterinary technician said.
"I guess he's just like me!" cried Lizzie.
"He's got a disability. –

Now, can I take him home? -
Can I make him my own? -
He really makes me smile."
And Laurie said, "I knew he would, all the while."

Then everyone broke out in song,
Each one singing all along -
"I love my little Skippy,
Oh, yes I do,
I love my Skippy,
'Cause he's true blue!"

And everyone said in unison,
"It was really worth the ride!"
And even Skippy smiled,
As did Charlie in the Heavenly sky.

SKIPPY SAVES THE DAY

There once was a kitty named Skippy,
Who was owned by an old-town hippie.
One day, the hippie lost his way,
Since his long hair had blocked the view from his face,
And he fell into a construction hole in the road,
Was hurt, and passed away the same day.

So the hippie had made no plans for his Skippy
To go to another home of a friendly home-town hippie,
So when his landlord came 'round,
Little Skippy he found -
To whom he did something mean:
He turned Skippy out into the street.

Now, a little girl was passing by,

When she heard poor, little Skippy cry.

And she went to investigate,

Hoping - to take the kitty home post haste!

(You see, her older brother - her best, best friend,

Had left for college - far away.

Leaving her without her playmate.)

Now Skippy was glad to assume the role
Of new best friend to Adelaide,
'Til her brother came home from college in May,
Because Adelaide thought Skippy was GREAT!
And that is how Skippy saved the day.

ABOUT THE AUTHOR

Born and educated in Massachusetts, Miss Kelleher began her undergraduate studies in the Liberal Arts at prestigious Wheaton College in Norton, where she was on the Dean's List. A transfer student, she received the degree of "Bachelor of Arts with Distinction" from Simmons College, Boston. Graduating in the top five percent of her class while majoring in Sociology, Economics and Art History, beyond "Distinction" additional baccalaureate honors conferred included: Academy (Collegiate Honor Society), Departmental Recognition (History of Art), Dean's List and receipt of academic grants.

Further general art historical studies and specialized new directions reflecting a burgeoning interest in American Art and Culture as well as European Painting of the Nineteenth Century, were undertaken within the Department of the History of Art, Master of Arts and Doctor of Philosophy program at Boston University's Graduate School of Arts and Sciences. By age twenty-four, she had independently researched and authored her first book and the first art historical book ever written on Boston artist, Lilian Westcott Hale - titled *Enchantment: The Art and Life of Lilian Westcott Hale, America's Linear Impressionist.* A year later came the independently researched and written *Unlikely Icon* and the majority of *Sense, Sensibility and Sensation: The Marvelous Miniatures and Perfect Pastels of Laura Coombs Hills, America's Lyrical Impressionist.*

Eventually, new interests in English Literature beckoned, so Kelleher completed a Master of Arts Degree in English Literature at Clark University in Worcester, Massachusetts, where she received a full scholarship and wrote her book *The Rose Upon the Trellis: William Faulkner's Lena Grove.*

Currently enrolled in the Master of Science Degree in Business Administration at Worcester State University, Kelleher is pursuing business courses while editing her soon-to-be-published book on Laura Coombs Hills. She was also accepted to study at Clark University, having received the Clark Alumni Scholarship.

Her other five books include: *The Fantasmagorical Feline Adventures of Little Miss Libby; The Secrets of Willow Creek; How to Research, Write and Publish an Art History Book in American Art;* and *Unlikely Icon: The Art, Culture and Philosophy of Forest Hills Cemetery, Boston: A Nineteenth Century Symbol of American Values* and *Friendship Cottage: The Little House that Big Jack Built.*

She is the niece of the renowned Hollywood writer and producer, the late Paul W. Keyes of Paul W. Keyes Productions, Westlake Village, California.